Perspectives

Places People Live

When is a Home a Home?

Series Consultant: Linda Hoyt

Flying Start
to Literacy®

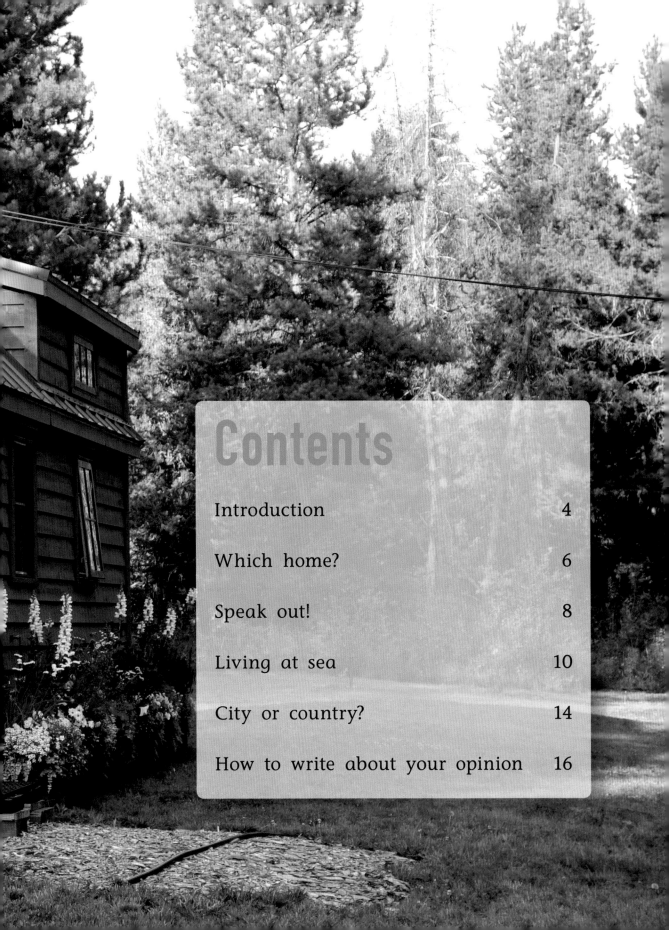

Contents

Introduction

What makes a home?

All people need a place to be safe from the weather, a place to keep their belongings, and a place to eat and sleep. This place is your shelter – it is your home.

Many people live in a house or an apartment. But some people live in different kinds of places: in treehouses, on boats, in homes under the ground or on stilts over water. For those who live in such a place, it is just their home!

What is your idea of what makes a home?

Which home?

If you could choose, which of these homes would
you live in? What is the same for each?
What is different?

Speak out!

Read what these students think is important about the places where they live.

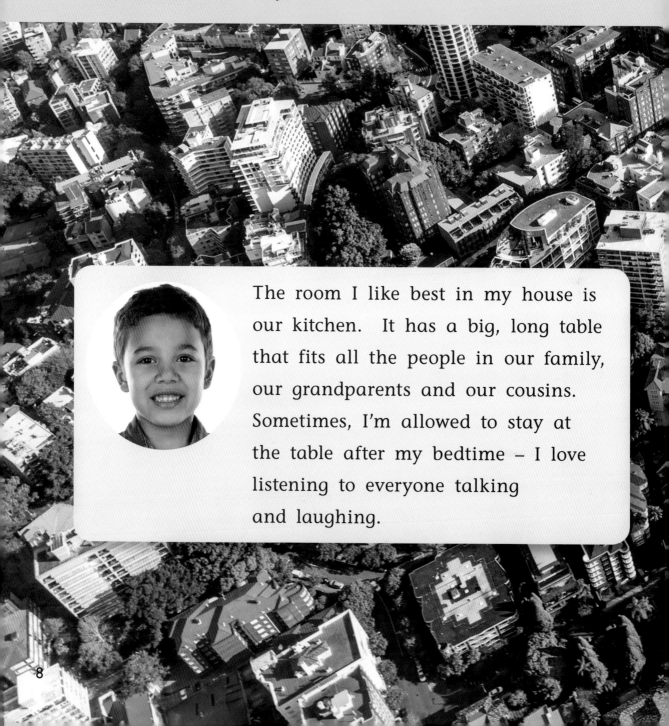

The room I like best in my house is our kitchen. It has a big, long table that fits all the people in our family, our grandparents and our cousins. Sometimes, I'm allowed to stay at the table after my bedtime – I love listening to everyone talking and laughing.

8

The place I like best at my house is the treehouse that my dad built for me when I was five years old. I love climbing up the ladder and looking down on the world – I can see all the way to the city.

A home doesn't have to be just four walls. It can be big, small, wide, square or triangular. You could be living outside and that could be a home.

You feel safe at home because of your family. The reason you feel safe at home is because you have your family with you and you know they will do anything to protect you.

Living at sea

Can you imagine living on a boat, moving around from place to place, with the ocean as your backyard? Well, for 10-year-old Eden Harrison and his family, this has been their life for the past two years.

Reporter Jessica Chan interviewed Eden about his unique home.

What do you think would be the good things and the bad things if you lived on a boat?

Q. What do you like about living on a boat?

A. I like that we move around a lot and we get to see many different places. I love snorkelling and exploring coral reefs. And it's exciting deciding what place we will visit next.

Q. What things are difficult about having a boat as your home?

A. It's very cramped. I have to share a small cabin with my sister. And sometimes, it's boring when we're out at sea for days and days when we travel long distances.

11

Q. What sort of food do you eat?

A. We eat a lot of fish, of course! When we go on land we buy fresh fruits and vegetables, as well as foods that will last longer, like pasta and rice.

Q. Do you miss seeing your friends every day?

A. Sometimes. But I get to play with other kids that live on boats. We meet them when we dock at ports in cities and towns. We have a lot in common, so it's easy to make friends quickly.

Q. Do you do school lessons on the boat?

A. Yes. Mum and Dad home school us. And we learn about other cultures by seeing how people live, hearing their languages and trying their food. So far, I have visited over ten different countries.

Q. How long will you live on the boat?

A. We're not sure. My sister is talking about going to university one day, so we might have to leave then. But for now, I don't want to live anywhere else.

City or country?

Some people live in big, busy cities. Some people live in the country, where there are fewer people and more space.

What about you? Are you a city person or a country person?

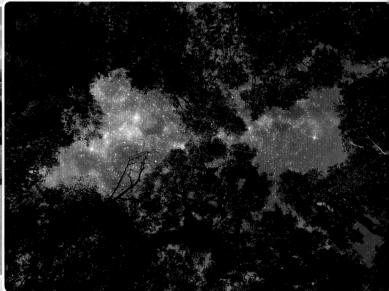

Jordan

"I live on a farm, on the outskirts of our town. We have lots of space to play outside. My sister and I go fishing, ride our bikes or climb trees.

When I want to play with my friends, I ride my bike to their house, or my friends ride to my house. My friends love playing on my farm. Best of all, we love camping out under the stars at night."

Chelsea

"I live in a big city, in an apartment on the 34th floor. Hundreds of people live in my building.

There are lots of great places to visit in the city. When my sister and I want to play outside, my dad has to take us to the park at the end of the block. There's often other kids from our building there, too. We always have a great time!"

How to write about your opinion

State your opinion

Think about the main question in the introduction on page 4 of this book. What is your opinion?

Research

Look for other information that you need to back up your opinion.

Related information book   Internet   Other sources
Incredible Underground Homes

Make a plan

Introduction

How will you "hook" the reader to get them interested?

Write a sentence that makes your opinion clear.

List reasons to support your opinion.

Support your reason   Support your reason   Support your reason
with examples.   with examples.   with examples.

Conclusion

Write a sentence that makes your opinion clear. Leave your reader with a strong message.

Publish

Publish your writing.

Include some graphics or visual images.